Wild Predators!

Deadly Spiders and Scorpions

Heinemann Library
Chicago, Illinois

Andrew Solway

Heinemann Library
...on of Reed Elsevier Inc.
...ago, Illinois

Customer Service   888–454–2279

Visit our website at www.heinemannlibrary.com

Design: David Poole and Paul Myerscough
Illustrations: Geoff Ward
Picture Research: Rebecca Sodergren,
Melissa Allison, and Pete Morris

Originated by Ambassador Litho Ltd
Printed and bound in Hong Kong, China by
South China Printing Co. Ltd.

09 08 07 06 05
10 9 8 7 6 5 4 3 2 1

**Library of Congress Cataloging-in-
Publication Data**
Solway, Andrew.
  Deadly spiders and scorpions / Andrew Solway.
    p. cm. -- (Wild predators)
  Includes bibliographical references (p.   ).
  ISBN 1-4034-5767-0 (hc : lib. bdg.) -- ISBN 1-
4034-5773-5 (pbk.)
  1. Spiders--Juvenile literature. 2. Scorpions--
Juvenile literature. I. Title.
  II. Series.
  QL458.4.S62 2004
  595.4'4--dc22
                              2004002148

Acknowledgments
The author and publisher are grateful to the
following for permission to reproduce copyright
material:
p. 4 E&D Hosking/Frank Lane Picture Agency; pp.
5 bottom, 18, 21 bottom C Nuridsany & M
Perennou/SPL; p. 5 top Stephen Dalton/NHPA; p.
6 Anthony Mercieca/SPL; pp. 7, 12 David
Fox/Oxford Scientific Films; pp. 8, 33 bottom
ANT Photo Library/NHPA; p. 9 Holt Studios; p.
10 Pascal Goetgheluck/SPL; pp. 11, 21 top
Daniel Heuclin/NHPA; pp. 13, 34 Anthony
Bannister/NHPA; p. 14 Minden Pictures/Frank
Lane Picture Agency; p. 15 Martin Dohrn/SPL;
pp. 16, 17, 32, 35 Ken Preston-
Mafham/Premaphotos; pp. 19, 22 John
Cooke/Oxford Scientific Films; p. 20 Gregory
Dimjian/SPL; p. 23 Susumu Nishinaga/SPL; p. 24
Silvestris Fotoservices/Frank Lane Picture
Agency; p. 25 Agence Nature/NHPA; p. 26 Frank
Lane Picture Agency/CORBIS; p. 27 Dr. Rod
Preston-Mafham/Premaphotos; p. 28 Dr. Samuel
Zschokke/SPL; p. 29 Ecoscene/CORBIS; p. 29 Rod
Planck/NHPA; p. 30 Dr. John Brackenbury/SPL; p.
31 William Ervin/SPL; p. 36 Stephen
Kraseman/NHPA; p. 37 top Dan Suzio/SPL; p. 37
bottom N A Callow/NHPA; pp. 38, 40, 41 bottom
Daniel Heuclin/NHPA; p. 39 Martin Harvey/NHPA;
p. 41 top Oxford Scientific Films; p. 42 Joe
McDonald/CORBIS; p. 43 Dick Jones/Frank Lane
Picture Agency.

Cover photograph of black scorpion reproduced
with permission of Daniel Heuclin/NHPA.
Title page photograph of an Argiope spider
reproduced with permission of PhotoDisc/Getty
Images.

Every effort has been made to contact copyright
holders of any material reproduced in this book.
Any omissions will be rectified in subsequent
printings if notice is given to the publisher.

The publisher would like to thank Paul Hillyard,
Curator of Arachnida at the Natural History
Museum, London, for his assistance in the
preparation of this book.

Contents

Eight-Legged Hunters

Although spiders and scorpions look very different, they are closely related. Both are arachnids (they belong to the class Arachnida). Both have a hard outer covering or exoskeleton, like insects. Both have eight legs rather than an insect's six. And both are very successful predators.

Spiders

There are about 38,000 known species of spider, and experts think that there are probably as many more to be discovered. Spiders live in almost every possible habitat, from high mountaintops to caves deep beneath the earth. Their main prey are insects. Many other animals eat insects, but spiders are by far the most effective insect predators.

Spiders have two parts to their body: a combined head and chest, known as the cephalothorax, and an abdomen (back part). As well as their eight legs, spiders have two small leg-like palps near the mouth. They use these for tasting, feeling, and handling things. The male also uses his palps for mating.

Spider silk

Some insects, such as silkworm moths, use silk to spin a cocoon, but only spiders produce such a variety of silk and use it in so many ways.

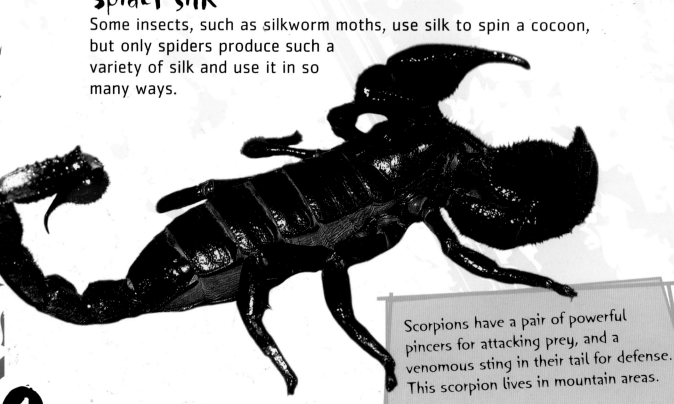

Scorpions have a pair of powerful pincers for attacking prey, and a venomous sting in their tail for defense. This scorpion lives in mountain areas.

Not all spiders spin webs like this European garden spider, but all use silk in several ways.

Nearly all spiders use strong silk as a safety line (dragline) to stop them from falling. Female spiders use a soft silk to wrap their eggs, and both male and female spiders use the same kind of silk to wrap their victims. Some spiders live in silk-lined dens or burrows. And web-weaving spiders use several kinds of silk in their webs.

All this silk is produced by the spider's spinnerets. Spiders have between two and six spinnerets at the back of their abdomen. Each one is like a tiny showerhead. It has hundreds of holes, all producing liquid silk.

Venomous fangs

A spider can use silk to catch prey, but it uses its jaws to subdue them. A spider's jaws end in long fang that are nearly always venomous.

Spiders use their venom to paralyze or kill their prey without a struggle, and to defend themselves. Most spider bites are not poisonous to people, but the venom of some spiders can injure or kill humans.

Liquid silk is pulled out of the orb weaver's spinnerets, either by gravity, by air currents, or by the spider moving away from the attached end of a thread. The pulling of the silk turns it from a liquid into a solid.

Stronger than steel

The dragline of the golden orb weaver spider is the strongest natural fiber known. It is stronger than steel and more elastic than nylon.

Giant Trapdoor Spider

The giant trapdoor spider has finished digging its burrow. It spins a silk lining, covering the inside of the burrow and the entrance. Next it cuts around the entrance hole to make a flap, leaving a hinge on one side. Carefully, it glues bits of soil to the flap, using sticky silk to hold them in place. The spider opens and shuts the trapdoor to test it. At last the burrow is finished.

Living fossils

Giant trapdoor spiders are found in southeastern Asia, China, and Japan. As their name suggests, these large spiders are over 4 in. (11 cm) across, including their legs.

Giant trapdoor spiders are considered living fossils. They are similar to spiders that lived over 300 million years ago. These primitive spiders do not build webs. Instead they dig a burrow using their powerful jaws, line it with silk, and make a trapdoor over the entrance.

Feeling the vibrations

Trapdoor spiders hide in their burrows and wait for prey to come along. Spiders can have as many as eight eyes, but despite this their eyesight is usually poor. Giant trapdoor spiders may have poor eyesight, but they are very sensitive to vibrations.

It takes a giant trapdoor spider six to twelve hours to make its burrow.

A giant trapdoor spider in threat posture. The photo shows the hairs all over its body that are sensitive to touch and vibration.

The giant trapdoor spider puts its front pair of legs against the trapdoor, and feels for the vibrations of a passing insect. When an insect comes close enough, the spider rushes out of the burrow, grabs its victim and retreats again, all in one smooth movement.

Some giant trapdoor spiders lay silken trip lines around their burrow. If an insect touches one of the lines, the spider feels it and rushes out. The lines extend the area where the spider can catch prey.

Finding a mate

Once a female giant trapdoor spider has built her burrow, she will stay there all of her life (usually one to two years). Males, however, must move around looking for the burrow of a female. When a male finds a female he enters the burrow, and if she accepts him they mate.

The female spider stores the male's sperm inside her body until she is ready to lay her eggs. She spins a mat of silk, lays the eggs, and deposits the sperm on them. Then she spins more silk around the eggs to make an egg case that she hangs up inside the burrow. After several weeks the eggs hatch, and the young spiderlings emerge. They stay in the burrow for a few weeks before leaving to dig their own burrows.

Sydney Funnel-Web Spider

A beetle scurrying beneath a rotting log stumbles over the trip lines around a funnel-web spider's lair. The spider rushes out to grab its prey. It lifts up its head and drives its large fangs vertically down into the beetle's body, like a pair of pick axes. Within seconds the venom in the fangs has done its work and the beetle is dead.

Deadly venom

The Sydney funnel-web spider is one of several funnel-web spiders found in southeast Australia. It lives in and around the city of Sydney. The male funnel-web spider is dangerous. Its powerful venom can make people seriously ill, and without medical attention a bite could kill.

The Sydney funnel-web is a brown to black spider with a body about 1 to 2 in. (2 to 5 cm) long. Funnel-web spiders like damp, cool, sheltered places, such as, under rocks or rotting logs, in crevices, garden rockeries, and dense bushes. Like giant trapdoor spiders, they dig burrows and line them with silk. But instead of a making a trapdoor, the funnel-web spider lays a tangled web of silk lines around the burrow entrance.

Sydney funnel-web spiders have downward-pointing fangs. Fangs like this are found only in mygalomorph spiders and giant trapdoor spiders.

Finding a mate

As with giant trapdoor spiders, female funnel-web spiders rarely leave their burrows. But males, once they are fully-grown, abandon their burrows to look for a female.

Males are attracted to a female's burrow by a scent that she produces. When a male finds a female's burrow he taps out a signal to the female. If she is ready to mate, she comes out and lifts up the front of her body, fangs ready to strike. If the male is not alert the female may make a meal of him. But he uses a pair of spurs (hooks) on his second pair of legs to hold on to the female's fangs, stopping her from striking. He is then able to mate with the female.

The tangle of silk lines spreading out from a Sydney funnel-web spider's burrow. The funnel-web's most common prey are beetles, cockroaches, and other insects.

Eggs and young

Soon after mating, the female spins a mat of silk on which she lays about 100 eggs. She then adds more silk to enclose the eggs in an egg case. The funnel-web spider hangs the case in her burrow, and about 3 weeks later the spiderlings hatch. They stay in the female's burrow for several months before leaving to make their own burrows.

Sydney funnel-web spiders take two to four years to mature. Males live only a few months as adults, but females can live ten years or more.

9

Tarantulas

The tarantula is as big as a man's hand; the viper is over 12 in. (30 cm) long. But the spider has the advantage of surprise. It dashes out of its burrow and buries its fangs in the snake's head. The snake tries to shake it off, but the tarantula hangs on. Soon the tarantula's venom takes effect, and the snake becomes quiet. The tarantula drags the snake back to its burrow and begins to eat.

Hairy spiders

Tarantulas are large, hairy spiders that live in warm areas around the world, including South America, southern North America, southern Europe, Africa, southern Asia, and Australia. Many tarantulas live in burrows, but they often take over the burrow of another animal rather than digging their own. Other tarantulas live in trees rather than in burrows. Most are active at night, when their poor eyesight is not a disadvantage.

Like funnel-web spiders, tarantulas are mygalomorphs. Their fangs are designed to strike downward, rather than working like pincers as in other spiders.

A magnified view of the hairs on the abdomen of a South American tarantula. Many tarantulas can fire off a cloud of hooked, highly irritating hairs if they are threatened.

The biggest spiders

One of the biggest spiders in the world is the goliath spider (*Theraphosa leblondi*). Its body can be 5 in. (12 cm) long, and including its legs it can measure 10 in. (25 cm) across. Goliath spiders live in coastal rain forests in South America. Because they are so large, some tarantula species hunt bigger prey than insects. They catch frogs, lizards, mice, and even small snakes. The tree-living tarantulas may also take young birds from their nests. This one has caught a mouse.

Eating prey

Although tarantulas have large jaws, they are not designed for chewing up prey. Like all spiders, tarantulas partly digest their food outside their bodies before eating it. Once their prey is dead or paralyzed, they inject or pour digestive juices into its body. Chemicals in the juices break down the prey's body tissues into a kind of liquid soup. The spider then sucks this up, using powerful muscles connected to its stomach. For a large animal such as a frog or lizard, this process can take up to a day.

Tackling threats

Tarantulas are large, but their bite is not very venomous, and many predators hunt them. As well as larger animals such as birds and lizards, they are attacked by some kinds of wasps. The wasps sting the spider to paralyze it, and then drag it to a burrow to provide food for their larvae.

Chilean rose hair tarantulas are often sold as pets. The Mexican redknee tarantula, another popular pet, may be endangered in the wild due to overcollecting for the pet trade.

Spitting Spiders

In the darkness it would not be possible for the spitting spider to see anything, even if its eyesight was good. But a breath of air tells it that an insect has landed not far away. Moving slowly and carefully, the spitting spider creeps closer. When it is about 1 in. (2 cm) away, it prepares to strike.

Two abdomens

Spitting spiders are small: they have a body only 0.12 to 0.24 in. (3 to 6 mm) long. Most species live in tropical regions, but one has spread around the world and is often found in houses. Spitting spiders are easily recognized because the front section of the body, the cephalothorax, is domed making the spider look almost as if it has two abdomens. Like other spiders, spitting spiders, have poor eyesight but an excellent sense of touch and vibration. They hunt by night and rest during the day.

Spitting glue

Spitting spiders rely on stealth to get close to their prey, creeping up until they are almost within an inch (few centimeters) of their victim. They then attack by spitting!

The cephalothorax of spitting spiders contains two venom glands. These glands produce venom as well as a sticky kind of silk.

One species of spitting spider has been carried around the world by the movements of ships, aircraft, and other transport. It is commonly found in houses.

Distant touch

Like other spiders, spitting spiders have hairs on their legs that are very sensitive to vibrations in the air. These hairs allow spiders to feel the air vibrations that are made when something moves at a distance.

When the spider spits, a stream of this sticky silk comes out of its fangs. As it spits, the spider vibrates its jaws from side to side, so that the spit comes out in two sticky zigzags; one from each fang. When the strings of spit hit the spider's victim, they glue it to the ground. Then the spitting spider moves in and gives the prey a killing bite.

The spitting spider is small, and its venom is not particularly powerful. By pinning down prey, such as this silverfish, with sticky spit, it reduces its chances of being injured.

A ball of eggs

Spitting spiders do not live in a burrow. During the day they find a safe resting place, such as a crack in a wall or under bark or stones. The female must find another way to keep her eggs safe. She does this by wrapping the eggs in silk to make a ball that she carries around in her jaws. The ball is large and awkward, but the female carries it for three weeks, until the eggs hatch. Once the spiderlings are born they are left to fend for themselves. They can live for two to four years.

Jumping Spiders

In a rain forest in Panama, a jumping spider is perched on a branch. About 1 ft (30 cm) away, a bee is collecting nectar from a flower. The jumping spider launches itself into the air, front legs extended, and lands on the bee. As it lands, its pincer-like fangs dig deep into the bee's back.

Active hunters

Jumping spiders are small, often colorful, and have excellent eyesight. They are active, alert hunters that do not use a web. Jumping spiders vary in size from about 0.12 to 0.8 in. (3 to 20 mm). They are found all over the world, but especially in tropical areas.

Telephoto eyes

The first thing that you notice about a jumping spider is its eyes. Jumping spiders have eight eyes, but one pair is much bigger than the rest. These large eyes act like a pair of binoculars.

A jumping spider's main pair of eyes give excellent vision, but only over a narrow area. The six smaller eyes enable the spider to see areas out of the view of the main pair. One pair is set wider than the main eyes; the other two pairs are set higher on the head.

Hunting tactics

Jumping spiders hunt during the day. At night they find a hiding place such as a crack to rest in. They are constantly on the move, looking around for the next meal.

A *Chrysilla* jumping spider's eyes. To make the best use of its main eyes, a jumping spider has a very mobile cephalothorax that can turn in any direction.

When a jumping spider spots prey, it does not attack right away. Like a stalking cat, it gets as close as possible before launching an attack.

By spider standards, jumping spiders are smart. When they stalk prey, jumping spiders often approach by a devious route. To do this they must work out at least part of the route beforehand. Such forward planning is exceptional among spiders.

A jumping spider never attacks without a dragline. It anchors the end of the line before it pounces, so that if it misses it simply swings from the dragline rather than falling. The dragline also has other uses. When the jumping spider's prey is big and strong, the spider will often dig in its fangs, then hang from its dragline. Hanging in midair, the victim can do nothing, and the spider's venom has time to work.

A Panamanian jumping spider launches itself at a cricket. The spider trails a dragline that connects it to a safe anchor point.

High jumpers

Two kinds of jumping spider have been found at heights of nearly 23,000 ft (7,000 m). At this height no plants grow, but plant material blown from lower down is enough to feed some tiny creatures, and the jumping spiders feed on these.

Making the leap

Although they try to get as close as possible to their prey, jumping spiders finally attack with a leap. They can leap up to 40 times their own body length. If a human could jump this far, they would be able to jump over 230 ft (70 m)!

Jumping spiders do not have strong muscles in their legs. They jump by contracting (tensing) muscles in their abdomen, which forces liquid into their back legs. The back legs straighten, and the spider is catapulted forward.

Courtship shows

Because jumping spiders have good eyesight, males can use visual displays to try to persuade a female to mate.

Male jumping spiders often look very different from the females. At one time, the males and females of some jumping spiders were thought to be different species. Male jumping spiders are often brilliantly colored, or they may have frills or fringes on their legs or abdomen. They show off their finery to females in a courtship dance. The male may wave his legs, lift up his abdomen, or display other parts of the body. If the female likes the male's display, she will allow him to mate with her.

Jumping spiders performing a courtship dance.

The fringed jumping spider looks like a dead leaf or a piece of garbage rather than a spider. Its strange looks are thought to confuse other spiders that don't recognize it as an enemy.

Eggs and young

Once the female has mated, she prepares a silk nest in which she lays her eggs. The nest is usually attached to a leaf, and can contain several hundred eggs. Some female jumping spiders guard their eggs until they hatch, but others make several nests, and guard none of them. When the spiderlings hatch they are small, but able to look after themselves. Predators such as centipedes, ants, birds, lizards, and even other spiders eat many of the spiderlings.

Fringed jumping spider

The fringed jumping spider (also called Portia, from its scientific name) lives in woodlands and rain forests in Australia and southeast Asia. Portia likes to eat other spiders, especially web-builders. Most spiders cannot walk on another spider's web without getting entangled, but Portia seems to manage with ease on a wide variety of webs. It is also extremely cunning. When Portia enters a web, it uses its legs to vibrate or tap on the web. The vibrations make the resident spider think that it has caught prey, and it rushes out to investigate. But Portia leaps on its victim before the other spider knows what it is dealing with. Portia can do this because its superb eyesight is even better than that of other jumping spiders.

Crab Spiders

A crab spider sits motionless on a flower, front legs held wide, waiting for prey. It is almost invisible, its white body matching the petals of the flower. A butterfly lands on the flower, and the crab spider grabs it with its spiny front legs. The butterfly struggles briefly, but the spider bites it on the back of the neck and the fast-acting venom soon makes the butterfly still.

Plant spiders

There are over 2,000 different species of crab spider around the world. Crab spiders live on plants and catch insects that come to feed. Most are small spiders with bodies less than 0.4 in. (1 cm) long.

Crab spiders are like crabs in several ways. Their bodies are flattened like a crab's, and they hold their longer front two pairs of legs out to the sides like a crab's claws. Crab spiders also move like crabs, with a sideways scuttle. Finally, a pair of the crab spider's eight eyes is on short stalks, like a crab's eyes.

Blending in

Crab spiders are masters of camouflage. Different species are colored and shaped to blend in with the kinds of plants upon which they are usually found.

This flower crab spider blends in perfectly with the flower that it is sitting on. Some crab spiders can change color to match their background.

Masters of disguise

Not all crab spiders mimic flowers. Some conceal themselves on leaves or plant stems. The bark crab spider is colored like bark. One group of spiders even mimic bird droppings!

As well as helping it to ambush prey, a crab spider's disguise hides it from predators such as birds and mantids that might find a spider a tasty mouthful. Some crab spiders look remarkably like ants. This disguise is a good protection against enemies, because few predators attack ants. Ants have a fierce bite and can spray unpleasant acid chemicals at any attacker.

Tying up its mate

Male crab spiders are smaller than the females. When they want to mate with a female, they tie her down with strands of silk. The silk is not really strong enough to hold the female if she wanted to escape. But the tying process calms the female, and makes it safe for the male to mate with her.

After mating, the female lays her eggs. Some flower spiders lay their eggs on a leaf, then curl it around like an ice cream cone. The female stands guard over the eggs for 2 weeks without eating, and dies after they hatch.

A female crab spider and a much smaller male. When females are ready to mate they are thought to send out a scent. Males are attracted by the smell, and follow it to find the female.

Wolf Spiders

The female wolf spider has been carrying the egg case for weeks. Now the young are ready to hatch. The female takes the egg case and bites a row of perforations (tiny holes) all around the edge. Soon, a stream of tiny spiderlings swarms out of the egg case and onto their mother's back.

Good eyesight

Wolf spiders are a family of medium to large spiders. The biggest wolf spider has a body length of up to 2 in. (4 cm). These ground-living spiders are found in a wide range of habitats around the world. Like jumping spiders, wolf spiders have excellent eyesight.

A wolf spider's eyes are arranged in three rows: a lower row of four small eyes, a middle pair of large, forward-facing eyes, and another pair of medium-sized eyes high on the head.

Sit-and-wait hunters

Wolf spiders usually find their prey by sitting in a concealed spot and waiting. Once a victim comes near, the wolf spider chases it down. Wolf spiders sometimes even leap into the air to catch a flying insect in their front legs before giving it a venomous bite.

Male displays

Because their eyesight is good, male wolf spiders try to impress females with visual displays. Males usually have markings or hairs on their palps or front legs, to make them stand out. The male waves his palps or legs in a jerky courtship dance to try and persuade the female to mate.

Wolf spiders carry their egg cases on their spinnerets, so they can continue to hunt. Some other spiders carry the egg cases in their jaws, which means they cannot eat while the eggs are developing.

Caring mothers

After mating, the female lays her eggs in a shallow hammock of silk, and shapes them into an egg case like a ball.

The eggs take several weeks to hatch, during that time the female carries the egg case around. If the weather is good she will sometimes sit in a sunny spot to warm the eggs. This helps them to develop more quickly.

When the eggs hatch, the baby spiderlings hitch a ride on their mother's back. After about a week, when the young spiders shed their first skin (molt), they leave their mother and start to hunt for themselves.

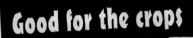

Good for the crops

Wolf spiders are helpful to farmers, because they feed on pests, such as caterpillars that eat crops. But insecticides that are sprayed on crops to control pests kill the helpful spiders as well. Using insecticides sparingly and only when needed allows spiders to thrive and helps protect crops from damage.

Wolf spiderlings on their mother's back. They do not need to eat until after their first molt, but their mother may let them off her back to drink.

21

Wandering Spiders

Picking up his shoes, the man sees a movement in one of them and drops it. A large brown spider falls out, looking very agitated. The man grabs a broom from the corner of the room and tries to push the spider out of the door. But the spider leaps on the broom and runs up the handle. With a yell, the man drops the broom and rushes out of the room.

A Brazilian wandering spider has large eyes and red jaws. The eyes are arranged differently than those of wolf spiders.

Night hunters

Wandering spiders are medium to large spiders that look similar to wolf spiders. Most kinds are found in tropical areas, especially rain forests, but the Brazilian wandering spider is often found around places where people live. Wandering spiders are more active hunters than wolf spiders. They hunt at night and actively stalk their prey as well as sitting and waiting for them. Because they are night hunters, they rely on hearing, sensing vibrations, and smell, rather than eyesight.

Finding a mate

When a male wandering spider is looking for a female to mate with, he follows the smell of chemicals she releases. The female attracts males by laying down strands of silk with a special scent. When a male finds a female, he vibrates the leaves of the plant upon which she is sitting. The female responds with her own vibrations if she is ready to mate.

Like wolf spiders, female wandering spiders carry their egg cases on their spinnerets, but they do not protect the spiderlings once they have hatched.

Brazilian wandering spider

Brazilian wandering spiders are about 5 in. (12 cm) across, including their legs. During the day Brazilian wandering spiders rest under fallen trees, in bunches of bananas, or in bromeliads (large plants that grow on tree branches). They sometimes wander into houses and hide away in shoes or under furniture. Unlike most spiders they do not run away when disturbed, but stand their ground or attack.

The Brazilian wandering spider has extremely powerful venom and is one of the most dangerous spiders in the world. Its bite causes great pain, and can be fatal to humans unless treated promptly.

Active hunters, like jumping spiders and wandering spiders, have "sticky feet." Each foot ends in two claws, and between them is a tuft of fine hairs. These hair tufts give the spider excellent grip—even upside down!

Rusty wandering spider

Rusty wandering spiders are very large wandering spiders found in the rain forests of Costa Rica. Adults may be 6 in. (14 cm) across, including their legs. Like the South American tarantulas, these wandering spiders hunt tree frogs and lizards. They hone in on tree frogs through their croaking that the spiders hear through sense organs on their legs.

Water Spider

The spider is brown, but it has a silvery sheen because of the air bubbles trapped around its body. It swims vigorously toward the surface of the pond where it lives, where a small fly is struggling to escape from the water. The spider grabs the fly and pulls it down to its underwater den.

Water specialists

Water spiders live in ponds, lakes and slow-moving rivers in temperate areas of Europe and Asia. They measure between 0.28 to 0.75(7 to 19 mm) long.

Water spiders are the only spiders that spend their whole lives in water. Their bodies are covered in fine hairs that trap air bubbles. They build themselves an underwater air supply similar to an air-filled diving bell.

Making a diving bell

A water spider begins making a diving bell by spinning a sheet of silk underwater that it attaches to the stems of water plants. Then it swims to the surface to collect some air. It does this by sticking its back legs out of the water and trapping an air bubble between its legs and its abdomen.

A water spider carrying an air bubble to its underwater den. The tiny hairs on its legs and body help to trap air.

The water spider now swims down and releases the bubble of air underneath its sheet of silk. The air bubble remains trapped underwater. After several more trips, the spider's diving bell is complete. From time to time the spider will collect more air from the surface, as supplies in the bell run low.

Female water spiders make a large bell and wait for prey inside it. Males build smaller retreats and spend more time outside them, hunting prey more actively.

Bringing up young

Male and female water spiders mate underwater in the female's diving bell. After mating, the female makes another diving bell where she lays her eggs and makes an egg case to hold them. The female stands guard in this diving bell until the eggs hatch. After hatching, the spiderlings stay in the diving bell for about 25 days. They are then ready to make a diving bell of their own.

Water spiders take prey back to their diving bell to eat it. They hunt small fish and water creatures as well as insects at the surface.

Marine spiders

Although they do not live underwater all the time, some wolf spiders can also survive in water. One kind, the marine wolf spider of Australia, lives half of its life in the ocean. This spider lives in and around rock pools, feeding on small fish and crustaceans. When the tide comes in, the spider climbs into a rock crevice and spins a web of silk over the entrance. It stays in this snug retreat until the tide goes out again.

Sheet-Web Spiders

A tiny spider hangs upside down beneath a hammock-shaped sheet of closely woven silk. Above the sheet is a tangled scaffold of silk lines, designed to trap unwary insects. The spider feels a vibration: an insect is on the scaffold lines. The spider shakes the web and the insect falls onto the sheet. Running quickly over the underside of the sheet, the spider bites, injecting venom into its victim.

Web builders

Spiders are the only group of animals to build webs. Webs are silken traps designed to catch flying or crawling insects. Over millions of years, webs have evolved into a variety of different kinds, including, sheets, tangles, cobwebs, ladder webs, and the elegant orb web.

The most common web-building spiders in temperate parts of the world are sheet-web, also known as money spiders. Sheet-web spiders are between 0.04 and 0.20 in. (1 and 5 mm) long. They weave small sheet webs with a tangled scaffold of lines above. The webs of these spiders are not sticky. They rely on their tangled scaffold lines to trip up walking insects and bring down flying ones.

A sheet-web spider hanging from its web, waiting for prey.

A spider preparing to take to the air. Usually spiders travel only short distances by air, but they have been found at heights of 15,000 ft (4,500 m) and 994 mi (1,600 km) from the nearest land.

Mating and young

Sheet-web spiders live for less than a year: they are born in spring and die in late fall. As soon as they are adults, sheet-web spiders mate. Males look for a female who is not quite mature. When a male finds such a female he stays with her until she becomes a full adult and is ready to mate. During his stay he may have to fend off other males that are looking for partners.

Once she has mated, the female begins producing eggs. She lays them in batches in hiding places such as under leaves, wrapping each batch in an egg case. The female dies in the winter, but most of the eggs survive the cold and hatch the following spring.

Spider balloonists

If the numbers of sheet-web spiders in an area get too large, some may decide to leave and look for somewhere better to live. They do this by ballooning. To balloon, a spider climbs to the top of a plant or other high place, and turns to face the wind, its abdomen lifted. It then releases a strand of silk that gets longer as it is pulled out by the wind. When the strand is long enough, it lifts the spider into the air. Most other spiders are too heavy to balloon as adults, but they often do so when young.

Garden Spider

The garden spider sits in the center of its web, alert for any sign of prey. A sudden vibration tells it that an insect has crashed into the web. The spider hurries up to its struggling victim and wraps it quickly with a broad band of silk. Then it finishes the prey off with a bite.

Orb-web weavers

When most of us think of a spider's web, we think of an orb web. The orb web is designed to catch flying insects. The garden spider is the best known orb-web weaver. Garden spiders are common in northern parts of the world, but there are also many other kinds of orb weaver.

Building a web

Each morning, a garden spider spins a new web. First, it lets out a fine silk line on the breeze until the line sticks to a nearby object. Then it runs across this line trailing another, stronger thread. From the center of this thread, the spider drops down onto another thread that it attaches to a third point. The two lines now make a *Y* shape (the first line is pulled down into a *V* by the second one). The center of the *Y* becomes the center of the web, and the spider attaches more lines radiating out from this central hub.

This computer drawing shows the path of a spider building its web. The first Y-shape is shown in red, the threads spreading out from the center are in yellow, and the spiral thread is shown in blue.

Garden spiders sometimes hide near their web and keep in touch through a signal thread. This thread vibrates if something lands on the web.

Now the garden spider lays another thread, running spirally outward from near the center of the web (a small area in the middle is left free). The outward spiral forms a guide for a second spiral thread that the spider lays from the outside inward. This thread is sticky, and replaces the guide spiral (the spider cuts out the first spiral as it puts in the new one).

The web is now complete, and the garden spider can settle on the web to wait for a victim.

Yellow garden spider

The yellow garden spider is a large orb-web spider found in North and Central America. Yellow garden spiders often add zigzags of heavier white silk to the web. Experts think that they might be needed to strengthen the web, or that they are there to make the web more visible to stop birds from flying into it.

29

Golden Orb Weavers

From a distance it looks as if the bird is frozen in midair, its wings closed. But as the girl gets closer she sees that the bird is trapped in a huge spider's web, taller than she is. The bird is struggling feebly to escape, but it is exhausted. As the girl watches, a large spider appears and moves toward the bird.

The biggest webs

Golden orb weavers are a group of large spiders found in tropical areas around the world. Their webs are probably the biggest and strongest of any spider. They can be 7 ft (2 m) or more across. These huge webs are built by the females that can have a body 3 in. (7 cm) long.

Unlike garden spiders, golden orb weavers do not take down their webs each evening, but repair them when they get damaged. The main prey of golden orb weavers are large flying insects. Once a victim is caught in the web, the orb weaver rushes in and bites it, then carefully wraps it in silk before carrying it away to eat in a sheltered place.

Tiny males

In many golden orb weaver species, the males are very small. They can be as little as 0.20 in. (5 mm) long and weigh hundreds of times less than the female. In other spider species, males have to be careful that the female doesn't eat them for lunch. But golden orb weaver males have no such worries. They are hardly worth eating!

Golden orb weavers get their name from the golden yellow sheen of their webs.

Communal webs

A female's web usually has several males on it. They compete with each other for the best position to mate with the female – in the center of the web.

Once the female has mated, she leaves her web to find a sheltered place to lay her eggs (often under leaves). Here she spins an egg case around her eggs. She does not guard the eggs, but goes back to her web. After a few days the egg case turns green and becomes almost invisible against the leaves.

The eggs hatch after two to three months. The newly hatched spiderlings stay together for a time and spin a communal web. After a few weeks they separate to build their own webs.

Male golden orb weavers are tiny in comparison to the giant females.

Useful spiders

Humans around the world have found several uses for golden orb weaver spiders. In the past in New Guinea, hunters used the webs of golden orb weavers as fishing nets. In Laos, in Southeast Asia, people eat these large spiders. And scientists in The United States Defense Department are trying to copy golden orb weaver silk in order to use it for bulletproof vests.

Net-Casting Spiders

All day the spider has been perched motionless on a branch, looking like a broken twig. Now as darkness falls, it begins to build its web. First it makes a simple scaffolding of thin threads. In the center is an area the size of a postage stamp. Now the spider lays dense strands of white silk across this area to form a small net. As it lays down each strand, it uses its back legs to comb the silk, making it fluffy like wool.

Smaller webs

Spiders use up a lot of energy producing silk. To save energy, some web-building spiders have found ways to hunt with a much-reduced web. One group of spiders that have done this is the net-casting spiders.

Net-casting spiders have stick-like bodies 0.79 to 1 in. (2 to 2.5 cm) long and long, thin legs. They are found worldwide in tropical areas.

Net-casting spiders are also called ogre-eyed spiders, because their two front eyes are so enormous. They need such large eyes because they hunt for prey at night. Their eyes are designed to collect as much light as possible.

A net-casting spider poised to catch a victim in its net.

Casting the net

At night, the net-casting spider spins its small, elastic net. The spider then lowers itself to hang upside down, holding the corners of the net-web in its four front legs. When an insect passes below, the spider lunges downward, scoops up the insect in its net and springs up again. It then wraps its victim in extra silk and gives it a venomous bite. Net-casting spiders catch beetles, ants, crickets, spiders, and even moths in this way.

The web-casting spider's net is not sticky, but is made of jagged silk. This is very fine silk that has been combed into fluffy strands that entangle the legs of an insect.

A web with one thread

Bolas spiders have reduced their web to just a single thread. They are named after the bola, a throwing weapon used by South American cowboys to catch animals.

Bolas spiders hunt at night for particular kinds of moth. Their web is a long thread with a sticky ball of silk on the end. The silk has the scent of a female moth and it attracts male moths. When the spider feels a moth close by, it swings its web around until the sticky blob hits the moth. The spider then reels its victim in.

An Australian bolas spider swings its thread. Bolas spiders are also found in the United States and Africa.

Social Spiders

A large grasshopper crashes into the sheet web and becomes trapped by the woolly silk lines. As it struggles to free itself, a large group of spiders rushes up from different directions. The spiders swarm over the grasshopper, biting it repeatedly. Soon it is dead, and the spiders settle down together to eat it.

Living in groups

Most spiders live alone, and only meet other spiders when they mate. However, a few species of spider are social, which means they live in groups. Most of these social spiders are found in tropical areas, where there are plenty of insects to feed on year-round.

Social living can have several advantages. There is safety in numbers. Spiders in a large colony are safer from predators than they are alone. A group of spiders can also kill much bigger prey than a single spider on its own.

Spiders working together can also make and repair webs more efficiently, and a large communal web improves the chances of catching insects. Easier web repair is perhaps important in tropical areas, where heavy rainstorms often damage spiders' webs.

In Africa, the webs of social spiders such as *Stegodyphus* colonies can grow to cover whole trees. In India the webs may cover vegetation for many miles (kilometers).

Stegodyphus spiders

Stegodyphus spiders are one group of social spiders that are found in Africa, India, and South America. They build webs rather like tennis nets, strung between two attachment points. At one end of the web is a ball-shaped nest. A colony (group) of *Stegodyphus* spiders can start with just a pair of spiders. As the numbers in the colony grow, the ball-shaped nest becomes bigger, and the webs spread over an increasing area. Most of the spiders born in the colony are female. With more females the colony can grow more quickly, and produce other colonies to spread over the area.

During the day most of the spiders stay in the nest away from predators, but a few remain on the webs, waiting for prey. When a large insect lands on the web, the nearest spider signals to the others and a group quickly gathers to kill the prey. They will then drag it into the nest to eat, although at night they usually eat the victim on the web immediately.

Tiny squatters

The large webs of social spiders often have other spiders and insects squatting in them and living off prey caught in the webs. One tiny spider (*Uloborus ferokus*) lives its whole life in the webs of *Stegodyphus* spiders in India. It feeds on insects that are too small for the *Stegodyphus* spiders to bother with.

Black Widow Spider

An insect is crawling through a woodpile when it comes across a forest of vertical threads. The insect touches one of the threads and becomes stuck. As it struggles to escape, the thread comes loose from the ground and springs upward. The insect is stranded in midair. A black widow spider reels it in for the kill.

Widows, buttons, and red-backs

The female black widow is about 0.4 in. (1 cm) long. She is black and shiny, with a red hourglass shape on the underside of her abdomen. Males are much smaller—about 0.2 in. (4 mm), with yellow and red bands and spots on the abdomen.

Black widow spiders are found in many of the warmer parts of the world. The black button spider in South Africa and the red-back spider in Australia (which has a red stripe down its back) are both close relatives of the black widow.

Dangerous bite

The black widow is best known for its venomous bite. In the United States, about half of all cases of spiders biting humans are due to black widows. The bite can be extremely painful, and can cause muscle spasms and sickness for a week after being bitten. Only the female's bite is dangerous.

The venom of a female black widow kills prey quickly. This avoids any chance of the spider being injured by a struggling victim.

Black widows can occasionally catch mice, lizards, snakes, and scorpions in their strong tangled webs.

A tangled web

The web of a black widow spider looks like a tangle, but it does have a structure. At the top are supporting threads. The web hangs from these. Below is a section of tangled threads where the spider waits for prey. Below this are the vertical trap threads that catch prey walking on the ground.

Only female black widows build webs and catch prey. Males do not feed as adults. They concentrate all their efforts on trying to mate with a female. When a male finds a female black widow's web, he taps on the web to signal that he is not lunch. Even so, after mating the female does sometimes eat the male. In red-backed spiders, the female begins feeding on the male while they are still mating!

Once the female has mated, she can produce eggs for the rest of her life (about two years). Every few weeks she lays a batch of several hundred eggs that she wraps in an egg case and hangs in her web. When the eggs hatch, the spiderlings leave home by ballooning.

Enoplognatha ovata are smaller relations of the black widow. They are fearless in taking on large or dangerous insects.

37

Scorpions

Scorpions are among the oldest kinds of land animals: they first crawled onto land over 300 million years ago. Like spiders, scorpions have 2 parts to their body, 8 legs and a strong outer covering (an exoskeleton) rather than bones inside their bodies. However, unlike spiders, they have a pair of large, crab-like pincers and an armor-plated abdomen divided into 7 segments (sections). And on the end of their abdomens scorpions have long, curving tails ending in a venomous sting.

Scorpions are nocturnal hunters that mostly feed on insects, spiders, and other invertebrates. Some larger scorpions also catch lizards, snakes, and mice. Many scorpions hunt by waiting in a burrow for prey, but some are more active hunters. Except in a few species, a scorpion's powerful pincers, rather than its sting, are their main weapons in catching prey.

The majority of scorpions are found in hot, dry parts of the world, but they can also be found in a range of other habitats, including grasslands, forests, rain forests, and caves.

Imperial scorpions (*Pandinus imperator*) are among the biggest scorpion species. This one is eating a Cameroon snake.

Giant ancestors

About 400 years ago, close relatives of the scorpion were swimming in the world's shallow seas and rivers. Some of these sea scorpions reached more than 7 ft (2 m) in length. They were among the biggest of all arthropods.

38

Glow in the dark scorpions

Nocturnal animals are hard for biologists to study because it is difficult to track their activities in the dark. However, scientists studying scorpions have found that they have an unusual property that makes tracking them at night much easier. Scorpions' bodies fluoresce (give out light) when lit with ultraviolet light. The scorpions give out an eerie green glow that makes them easily visible in the darkness.

Scorpion senses

Although a scorpion can have as many as twelve eyes, scorpions rely much more on their sense of touch and feeling of vibrations for finding and catching prey. Fine hairs on their pincers and body detect movements and vibrations in the air, while other sense organs on the legs feel vibrations through the ground.

Scorpions have one sense organ that is found in no other animal. Pectines are sense organs on the underside of the scorpion that look like two combs. They are thought to detect vibrations and chemical scents.

Vicious venom

The best known scorpion species are those that live in deserts. This is probably because some desert scorpions have an extremely venomous sting that can be fatal to humans.

Many kinds of scorpion dig burrows, either to rest in or to hunt from. This sand-burrowing scorpion has heavy pincers for digging in hard ground.

Death Stalker Scorpion

The scorpion picks up the scent of another scorpion in the sandy soil, and follows it to a burrow. A second scorpion comes out of the burrow, and the first one begins to shudder and shake. Then it grabs hold of the second scorpion's pincers in its own and hits the second scorpion with its tail. This is not a fight between two scorpions. It is a male and female beginning their mating dance.

Small pincers

Death stalker scorpions are about 4 in. (10 cm) long and colored yellow or orange. They are found in dry habitats in north and east Africa and the Middle East. Death stalkers hide in the abandoned burrows of other animals or under stones and wait for prey.

For most scorpions their pincers are their main weapons. Death stalkers have quite small pincers, but they have an extremely powerful sting that they can use to subdue large prey. Like most scorpions, death stalkers eat mainly insects, but will eat almost any prey of a suitable size that they come across.

A deadly sting

Death stalker scorpions belong to a scorpion family known as the Buthidae—the fat-tailed scorpions. Most of these scorpions have a thick tail and quite small pincers. Most of the scorpions with stings that are dangerous to humans belong to the Buthidae family.

The venom of death stalker scorpions is one of the most powerful found in any scorpion. Most people recover from a sting, but in a few cases it can be fatal.

The fat-tailed scorpions, which include the death stalker, are the biggest and most widespread scorpion family.

Apart from their sting, scorpions are also known for their mating dance. The male deposits a packet of sperm on the ground, and then takes hold of the female by the pincers and tries to move her over this sperm packet, so that she can take it into her body. Courtship dances can last from a few minutes to several hours. After mating is complete the male may make a quick getaway, but sometimes he is eaten by the female.

The female scorpion does not lay eggs; they develop inside her. This takes between 3 to 18 months, depending upon the species. The female gives birth to about 30 live young on average, although there can be as many as 100.

Young scorpions ride on their mother's back for the first twelve days or so. In most species the young then leave, but in death stalkers the mother and young may live together for a time.

Emperor Scorpion

The emperor scorpion sits motionless in its burrow deep in the African rain forest. There is a tiny vibration through the ground as a large beetle scurries past the burrow entrance. The scorpion shoots out of the burrow, and in a moment has crushed the beetle's hard outer shell in its powerful claws. It drags the beetle's remains into its burrow to feed.

Burrowing scorpions

Emperor scorpions are chunky black scorpions with large, heavy pincers. Death stalker scorpions live in dry areas, but emperor scorpions prefer the damp rain forests of western and central Africa.

Emperor scorpions belong to the burrowing scorpion family (Scorpionidae). All of these scorpions have heavy pincers for digging. Their pincers are powerful enough to crush small prey such as insects, so their sting does not need to be so venomous. With larger prey, such as lizards and mice, the scorpion may also sting its victim, and then use its pincers to hold onto it until the venom takes effect.

The sting of an emperor scorpion is similar in strength to a wasp or bee sting, but the scorpion can also give a serious nip with its pincers.

Biggest of all

Emperor scorpions are among the biggest of all scorpions. They can grow to a length of nearly 9 in. (23 cm). A scorpion found in India (*Heterometrus swannerdami*) is longer, measuring up to 11 in. (29 cm), but it is much slimmer and lighter than the emperor scorpion.

Long lived

Like death stalker scorpions, emperor scorpions have an elaborate mating dance. About 7 to 9 months after mating, the female gives birth to between 10 and 30 young. Emperor scorpions grow slowly and do not fully mature until they are about 18 months old. However, they also have a long life and can survive for 7 years or more in the wild.

Exotic pets

Experts do not recommend the keeping of scorpions as pets, but in recent years emperor scorpions have become popular as exotic pets. Emperor scorpions are not aggressive and their sting is not very dangerous to humans. There are some concerns that collecting these scorpions for the pet trade could threaten wild populations.

When pseudoscorpions need to get around, they hitch a ride on larger insects like this fly.

False scorpions

Pseudoscorpions (pseudo means false) are tiny relatives of scorpions and spiders. They look like tail-less scorpions but they are much smaller (the size of a grain of rice). They live in all parts of the world, hidden away under leaves, bark, or stones, feeding on even smaller creatures such as mites. The jaws of a pseudoscorpion produce silk. It uses this to spin a nest for protection during molting or over the winter. Although it does not have a sting, the pseudoscorpion's pincers are venomous.

Classification Charts

By comparing the characteristics of different living things, scientists can classify them (sort them into groups). A species is a group of animals or plants that are closely related. Similar species are put together in a larger group called a genus (plural genera). Similar genera are grouped into families, and so on through classes, orders, and phyla to the largest groups, known as, kingdoms. Spiders and scorpions are arachnids—part of the class Arachnida. Spiders are grouped in the order Araneae (true spiders), while scorpions belong to the order Scorpiones.

Order Araneae

There are about 38,000 known species of spiders. The main families are listed below.

Family	Number of Genera	Number of Species	Description or example
Giant trapdoor spiders (Liphistidae)	2	83	Malaysian giant trapdoor spider
Funnel-web spiders (Hexathelidae)	11	82	Sydney funnel-web spider
Trapdoor spiders (Ctenizidae)	9	114	Spiders that build burrows with a trapdoor over the entrance
Tarantulas (Theraphosidae)	107	860	Chilean rose-hair spider, goliath spider
Dysderids (Dysderidae)	24	480	Most common type has enormous fangs and lives on wood lice
Spitting spiders (Scytodidae)	5	157	Spitting spider
Daddy-longlegs spiders (Pholcidae)	68	779	Daddy-longlegs or huntsman spider
Uloboridae	19	244	Build horizontal orb webs; only spiders with no venom
Net-casting or ogre-faced spiders (Deinopidae)	4	56	Found mainly in tropics
Long-jawed orb weavers (Tetragnathidae)	56	983	Golden orb weaver
Orb-web spiders (Araneidae)	169	2817	Garden spider, yellow garden spider
Cobweb or comb-footed spiders (Theridiidae)	79	2199	Produce cobwebs often found in homes and buildings
Sheet-web weavers and dwarf spiders (Linyphiidae)	559	4214	Money spiders
Dictynidae	48	551	Water spider
Funnel weavers (Agelenidae)	42	489	Another family of funnel weavers: includes large, hairy house spiders
Wolf spiders (Lycosidae)	100	2261	Sharp-eyed hunting spiders
Wandering spiders (Ctenidae)	40	436	Brazilian wandering spider
Crab spiders (Thomisidae)	164	2023	Flower spiders
Jumping spiders (Salticidae)	538	4889	Fringed jumping spider (Portia)

Order Scorpiones

There are about 1,300 known species of scorpions. The main families are listed below.

Family	No. of species	Description or example
Buthids (Buthidae)	600	Death stalker and all most venomous scorpions
Scorpionids (Scorpionidae)	175	Emperor and other large scorpions
Vejovids (Vaejovidae)	125	Mostly desert or semi-desert species,
Bothriurids (Bothriuridae)	80	Found in burrows and crevices

Arachnid Bodies

Spider body parts

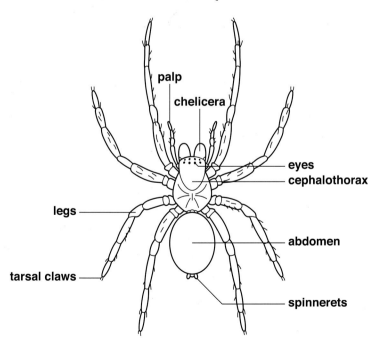

palp
chelicera
eyes
cephalothorax
legs
abdomen
tarsal claws
spinnerets

Scorpion body parts

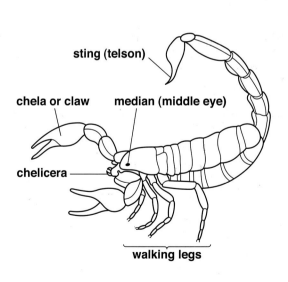

sting (telson)
chela or claw
median (middle eye)
chelicera
walking legs

Artwork
not to scale

Glossary

abdomen back part of the body of a spider or insect

arachnids group of animals that includes spiders, scorpions, and other related animals

arthropods animals that have a hard outer skeleton and jointed limbs. They include insects, spiders, and crustaceans.

ballooning in spiders, flying up into the air by letting out long loops of silk that catch the breeze

camouflage coloring and markings that help an animal blend in with its background

cephalothorax front part of a spider or scorpion's body

class large grouping used in the classification of living things. Mammals are a class of animals, as are arachnids.

cocoon protective silky case spun by some insect larvae

communal made or used by a group of animals or people

crustaceans group of mostly ocean-living arthropods, such as crabs, lobsters, and shrimp

digest break down food into nutrients that an animal can use for energy and growth

dragline safety line used by most spiders

endangered when an animal or plant species is in danger of dying out completely

evolution animals and plants evolve, or change slowly, over many years, to fit in better with their environment or compete better for food

exoskeleton tough outer skeleton found in all arthropods

fatal causing death

glands organs in the body that produce substances such as tears, saliva (spit), or venom

gravity force that pulls things toward the Earth

habitat place where an animal lives

invertebrate large group of living things, most of them small, that do not have a spine (backbone)

larva (plural larvae) young stage in the life cycle of an insect

mammal hairy, warm-blooded animal that feeds its young on breast milk

mantid (also called praying mantis) large predatory insect

mate when a male inserts sperm into a female animal to fertilize her eggs

mite small, spider-like creature closely related to spiders

molt spiders, insects, and some other animals have an outer skin that does not grow with them. When the skin becomes too small the animal molts (sheds its skin).

mygalomorphs spiders, such as tarantulas, that have downward-striking fangs

nocturnal active at night

palps leg-like feelers on either side of a spider's mouth. A scorpion's pincers are also a form of palps.

paralyze stun an animal so that it cannot move

predator animal that hunts and eats other animals

prey animal that is hunted by a predator

sense organs body parts specially designed for sensing, such as eyes, ears, etc.

species group of animals that are very similar and can breed together to produce young

sperm sex cells of a male spider or other animal

spinnerets silk-producing organs of a spider

temperate places where the climate is neither very hot nor very cold

trip lines silk lines laid along the ground where insects will stumble over them

ultraviolet high-energy light that humans cannot see

venom a poisonous liquid that spiders and scorpions inject into their prey to kill them. Animals that produce venom are venomous.

Further Reading

Halfmann, Janet. *Scorpions*. San Diego: Kidhaven, 2002.

Markle, Sandra. *Predators*. New York: Scholastic, 2003.

McGinty, Alice B. *The Black Widow Spider*. New York: Rosen, 2002.

Parker, Edward. *Insects and Spiders*. Chicago: Raintree, 2003.

Schwartz, David M. *Jumping Spider*. Milwaukee: Gareth Stevens, 2001.

Index